WHY I DIDN'T GO TO YOUR FUNERAL

COLIN POPE

Tolsun Books
Tolleson, Arizona & Las Vegas, Nevada

Set in Adobe Garamond Pro, 12pt font.
Design by David Pischke.

ISBN 978-1-948800-22-8

Published by Tolsun Books, LLC
Tolleson, Arizona & Las Vegas, Nevada
www.tolsunbooks.com

WHY I DIDN'T GO TO YOUR FUNERAL

POEMS BY COLIN POPE

ACKNOWLEDGEMENTS

Thanks to the editors of the following journals and publications, where some of these poems previously appeared (frequently in different versions):

Rattle, Barrow Street, Valparaiso Poetry Review, Poet Lore, The Healing Muse, Radius, Willow Springs, Connotation Press, Slate, Ninth Letter, Underground Voices, Texas Review, The Tulsa Voice, Harpur Palate, The Meadow, The Cortland Review, Juked, Pilgrimage, The Los Angeles Review, and *Constellations.*

"Dove Hunting" appears in the anthology *Wild Daisies from the Side of the Road: A Tribute to Maurice Kenny.*

"Keeping Appearances," "Gasoline Was a Trigger," and "Taking the Canoe Out at Night" appear in the anthology *The Burden of Light: Poems on Illness and Loss.*

Grateful acknowledgements to The Vermont Studio Center, The Academy of American Poets, The W. Morgan and Lou Clare Rose Trust, The L.D. and LaVerne Harrell Clark Literary Endowment, The Marye Lynn Cummings Scholarship Endowment, and the New York State Summer Writer's Institute for their generous support and encouragement, without which this manuscript would never have been completed.

I am thankful to the following people who helped in the making of this book. To my family, my colleagues, and my friends—thanks for your patience and your support. To my mother, who taught me how to survive. To Cyrus Cassells, Lisa Lewis, Roger Jones, Kathleen Peirce, Steve Wilson, Li-Young Lee, Terrance Hayes, Henri Cole, and the many teachers and mentors who believed in me and these poems. To David, Risa, and the wonderful people at Tolsun Books, who accepted and curated my work with such kindness, tenderness, and enthusiasm. Thanks to the Oklahoma State University and the Texas State University creative writing programs. And sincere thanks to those who helped me through my losses and recoveries and those who saw and worked on these poems, including John Andrews, Alysse Gopalakrishnan, Kate Click Williams, Melissa Cundieff, Andi McKay Boyd, Jason Rocha, Katie Markey, Kyle Hays, Jason Coates, William Jensen, Caitlin McCrory Evans, Amanda Perez, Shiloh Booker, Brandon Beck, Randy Kitchens, Clare Paniccia, Dustin Macormic, Cynthia Dewi Oka, and the many others who were there for me.

Very special thanks to Katie Ellison, my first and best editor. Thank you, thank you, thank you for loving me.

For George Wrisley, for the Kinneberg family, and for the rest of us survivors. This book is dedicated to the memories of Jennie and Lindsay Kinneberg. We miss you.

TABLE OF CONTENTS

But where are we,
Jenny darkness, Jenny cold?
Are we so old?
We came so early, we thought to stay so long.
But it is already midnight, and we are gone.

James Wright, "October Ghosts"

I

WHY I DIDN'T GO TO YOUR FUNERAL

Of course you didn't know what you'd made of me.
A blubbering focus, the frantic epicenter
around which soft hands gathered
to instruct and caress. For three weeks I moaned
and jerked like a carnival ride, owing visits,
wading an amaranthine stream of sorry, sorry,
sorry. Then I cleaned your house, took your dog,

proposed quiet solutions to the immobile planet
of your mother's head. When she said
I just can't would you go to the funeral parlor
and take care of things, I acquiesced.
Her voice a burned lampshade. Leaving the drive,
    the tires scratched and turned and

I couldn't tell who was being cared for anymore.
I didn't know if I cared. I witnessed the white
taken hold, blanketing you silent on the gurney
as that water left my eyes, uncontrolled,
a fact of pouring. You weren't autonomic

and then professional hands slid you into flames
to complete the notion that you couldn't exist.
    Oh, your friends came to the house,
stood in a clump beneath the railing from which
you'd dangled your noose. Daisies, I think,

tied with a string, and a picture that kept
blowing over, and nervous shoes in the dust.

It was ritual enough since you didn't exist
and the apologies had been stoppered up
as though there weren't enough left.
They were hoarding them now, the sounds
and letters having returned to simple shapes

like a face stared upon intently for too long.
    On the patio of a treehouse, a man said
he hated you and I tried to get mad.
But he meant it and I didn't, and we hugged
until my apathy returned again, warm
and cool and grey as a corpse. Fuck her,
he said. God damn her. Nod, I said. Look away

and nod, then walk to the car. You know I didn't
even send flowers to your service. Not a note or card.
I pillowed myself to the shape of a day
and waited for a head, which never came.
Nothing came. I would've gone to say goodbye
but I was all that was left. I drank instead.

HOW TO TELL IF A MOON
IS WAXING OR WANING

is one question you might ask while crying
as you lean your forehead against a picture window
or hover on the bank of a dumbstruck river
which wends off to places about which no one
could ever possibly care.

      Internalize, completely, why Meton of Athens
perched himself on a wicker chair in helpless silence—
432 BC—to catalogue lunar orbits and positions,
and his relief to discover time circles the heavens
via white shadow, every nineteen years, to restart

      the same day and date it began. Crater
by crater, it's easy to believe in god-magic and vaticination
when a crescent disappears like a face under water.
A sad prediction: you'll know someone who wants
to kill themselves, if you haven't already.

      They'll confess, abashed
and stuttering, because they care about you.
It will seem backwards. And then you can await
phasal shifts as this person oscillates between
yielding to pain and emerging from behind a black curtain

      invisible to the eye.
Nineteen years—that's Odysseus white-knuckled
on the foredeck of a ship, splashing toward a phantasm
something like home. That's the age by which

the first suicidal thought knocks on the night door

                              to ask, aloofly,
for your hand in marriage; like most of us you probably
contemplated jumping off a bridge, in the abstract,
or a mound of pills, tumbling down the throat.
Such is the difference, experts say, between a thought

                                        and
an ideation. For decades, archaeologists believed
the Paleolithic bone fragments found secreted
in the foothills of the Alps were dotted and marked
haphazardly, as though some idle caveman wiled away

bored hours on the first pointillism. Indeed, these the first
moon calendars, scrimshawed with scientific intent:
barefooted trails through the dust, a glancing
skyward intermittently to check if the moon would
still be there, fat and watchful as a nervous eye.

It's a planning, which takes memory; to ideate, one
must second-by-second remember they want to die.
The woman who spun me out into a whirl of tears waited
until the house was in careful sleep—her visiting mother,
cats,

even the neurotic poodle—before she tiptoed outside

to thread her noose over a low-hanging soffit. It took years
before I accepted how many feet, worldwide, shuffled
willfully to their own ends that night. In extremis
we glow important

beyond counting. Though some three thousand or so
other scintillas curlicued aimlessly into that dark beyond
dark, like solar flares averaged to a statistical recurrence,
I felt specific, reaching out for her one soul
thoughtlessly, the way a parent

throws their arm across a child just before the car
skids to stop short on the shoulder. But like astronomers,
they each soul charted a blank patch in the sky
and turned into nothing but theories of radiance
for theoretical generations—me—

to study. And if you're like me, it's time to ask
"who decides which theories are valid when none of them
ever work?" Okay, picture a guerilla war in the streets
of fifth century Alexandria between factions of solar
and lunar calendar acolytes. It happened: blood and light,

one half excising their months when the fingernail
of the waning moon was clipped clear off, the other
stretching upward to feel for gradients in warmth
like gibbons testing the air for God. I, too,
am terrified I'll evaporate into absence, and I just want

to know what matters. If you close your eyes
in a room with a clock, you can sense the hands
sweeping up after themselves, working to calculate
a remainder. We're gibbous to full, then crescent away,
then new, foolishly, when completely erased.

PACKING UP THE HOUSE

And then there were the books to consider,

lined smartly on the shelves,
piled on chairs, counters, coffee table,
hiding under the couch, a forgotten few
huddled in the closet by the water heater.
The boxes waited, confusing time

with their open mouths. Your father
thumbed a copy of *Tracking*
and the *Art of Seeing*. Your mother,
workmanlike, stopped to riffle the pages
of *The Hours*. She held the book close

and jumped, making a small noise, then
ran to me and said "Look! Look at this!
Do you think this *means* anything?"
You had underlined a passage in blue,
and she turned the full spotlight
of her face toward me, hoping.
The incense of paper hung in the air

as I studied the words, so far beyond
the reach of your mind, at that time
two days gone from the firm housing
of its brain. It was ten at night

and you lay on a cold table across town,
a suicide scheduled to be burned. I strained—
it took real effort—to find an expression
meant to look ponderous. "Yes," I finally said,

then turned away to tape another box shut.

THE NECESSARY

This is the moment when the ninety-year-old
turns in her white, white bed and asks me
what it's like to have an orgasm

and since she's never had one
and since the top floor of the hospice
is completely deserted this time of night

and since what question could really be
off limits at this point, I describe,
out loud, different things she should imagine:

riding a motorcycle, sprinting the orchard
with a shirt full of stolen apples, standing up
from the hot soil in the garden

when a breeze licks the sweat off your back.
Oh is that what it's like? she asks.
I guess not, I say. The droplets glitter

from the bag spike to the drip chamber
and into her veins, threading the clear outside
with the inner. To be honest I've never understood

more than I've witnessed: the arch of a spine
or tilt of hips or the reactive moans
that seemed to issue from the pure dumb luck

of my touch. It hurts for real, down to your core,
when you realize the cables and fiber-optics
are an invention, that the telepathies of pleasure

linking your senses with someone else's
were only a myth of your ego, which you hoped
you'd never see so exposed to open air.

She's grimacing a little and I want to give her this,
I want to tell her it looks kind of like
losing something inside yourself, searching for it,

but even that sounds stupid to me,
like a cruel ambiguity, like she could just lie down
and shut her eyes and seek out the seams

between one consciousness and another, that easy.
And I'd like to admit that I'm jealous of her,
for once in my life I'd like to confess

how much worse I am for the pursuit of sex,
overwhelmed by some Darwinian curse
like a male spider without a head.

But it's late. The janitor's cart chirps
up the hall and I'll never feel so clean.
Relax, I tell her. Close your eyes and breathe deep

and let's just see what we can do for that pain.

STILL LIFE WITH CASKET IN THE DISTANCE

We stood on the porch, marveling
at how little there was to do.
"I don't know what to say," someone said,

and I was not crying, you could not
call it crying, an ocean had simply tipped over
inside me and droplets were leaking out

from where my eyes used to be.
You couldn't really call them eyes, either,
for all the seeing they did not do

and I seemed to say, "It's okay, nobody has
to say anything." Like the angel of silence, I was.
Nobody made a sound. Someone I loved

was gone and it was hard to pretend,
it was foolish to be preoccupied by the business
of expression. A bird hollered overhead,

a car shushed by, the obscenity of its radio,
and everyone turned in wait, pregnant
for whether I'd explode or disappear

or clap my hands and deafen every ear
on the planet. Why do people die?
I kept wondering stupid things, fetal

as a question mark. I jammed my crowbar
between the teeth of every minute,
prying its mouth apart to see what it would say;

I couldn't believe how easily her final moment
had evaporated into the empty stratosphere
and I got very honest about lying. I'm going

to tell everyone the truth, I told myself,
I'm going to say it was a beautiful choice
and she made it well. Thankful: that's what

we should really be. Thankful is the word
loneliness loves, and we must be careful
only to say it to ourselves, the big bowl of it

gathering silence like a name no one
can quite remember. She didn't want this.
Not this railing to lean against, not all of us

lolling and scattered like apples in the grass.
We shine faintly without any reason to shine
or any knowing why we're put together.

SECOND EULOGY FOR A DROWNED BOY

We have it backwards, of course. Inflated
with reasons to stay alive,
we thrust armloads of meaning
upon these dead children. This one,

he doesn't care
and didn't even know his string had been yanked
clean off. *We wouldn't want to have died so young,*

is what we mean. *Before we knew enough*
not to die young. Like untying
the last balloon off a chairback

from the birthday yard. Yellow spot,
holding all that breath tight inside:
you can let it out now.
We just wanted to see what the clouds would do
when you bumbled across them. We can't imagine,

don't want to imagine
that moment they squeeze you so hard
in their soft, white embrace
you think you're home. What do you even know

of home? Glinting lid and shell,
the casket's crown as though it were stretched taut,
polished skin. What do you even know of home?
A blanket made

of a mother, draped across your chest,
shaking so violently she could pop.

IF YOU EVER BECOME A PAPER DOLL

After surviving the fanfold
and admiring your oblique body, don't be surprised
when a chain of perfect strangers

unfurl themselves from the raw material of you
and hold your hand. It's normal to be anxious
but if you're as good as you say you are,

you won't worry about who created whom
in whose image, or begrudge the loss of touch.
Or which one of you is the mother,

the father, which one came first.
Pray when the crayon touches your face
that the god of expression blesses you

with a smile, remembers the two small dots
for the eyes. Pray for shirt, for hair. Be thankful
you're not that poor, lonely twin

at the end of the line, one arm raised
and reaching out for someone
    who will never reach back.

"YOU ARE NOT YOUR EX-GIRLFRIEND'S MUSEUM."

These are the choices I'm given:
ignore or be ignored.
My mouth opens at the rim
of Yes, like walking around history.
It has happened, will happen,

and there's nothing to do but agree.
This collection is called *The Torture*
of the *Found Hairband.* This one

Weeping: A Retrospective. This,
A Survivor's Guide
to Smiling at Weddings and Parties.
At a bar, something like *So, tell me*

all about yourself
and the white heels of sunlight
scuff my marble floors.
A tour group departs on the hour.
My therapist says the window for closure

has closed, and now I have a city block
of grief to unpack and toothbrush clean.
Or neglected, slouching on a plinth,

the amphora that retains
remnants of me from the pre-
traumatic depressive era

will await a coughing patron's appreciation
in a distant, dusty wing. My therapist says

to throw everything in boxes
and store it in a closet or shed.
But without treasures,

what is a museum except white rooms
that chase each other in a circle?

There's a clipboard I'm using in my head.
I'm being catalogued, collected,
stored under glass. I have

future generations to consider,
gawkers with memories so short
they'd sell the dog inside the house

and the frame without the portrait
and the mummy right along
the dry, hackled emptiness
inside the sarcophagus. *I don't want,*

I say. *I need.* Beneath its surface,
desire is a choice. Those masters,
they'd paint one thing and then,

as though living two synchronized lives,
dip the brush heavy, slather the impasto

until a new dream obliterates
the beautiful stupidity
of what they thought they knew before.

ECHO

Is it wrong to say I'll mourn you forever?
One morning,
I mistakenly name my reflection "Jennie"
and it somehow sticks, like I'm a toddler
giving labels to the oddities of my surroundings
and nobody's there to correct me.

"Jennie" I say, two bloodshot eyes staring,
wildness in the hair, palms pressed flat
on the surface of the vanity.
For a moment it's unclear
whether I'm saying it, the person
I know myself to be, or Jennie is saying it,
the one in front of me,

speaker of her own name, adventurer
who's finally discovered the canyon's edge
and screams into its open mouth.

A LESSON WHILE HIKING MT. SKYLIGHT

for Maurice Kenny

Catkin, boscage, rumpled leaves like sun-yellowed pages

littering the rooms of an abandoned school.
That's how one might think of nature, Maurice:
as a student returning to a place

departed, not exactly certain it's been missed.
But I suspect you'd bristle at such a statement, reach back,

tighten the white column of your ponytail,
and explain *you can't miss what's forgotten*. Or, no,

something yet more human—that toothy, overbitten grin,
a little shake of your head as though clearing

the logjam of your thoughts to make way
for the truth. If you let the scrubby hillside
carry your descent to the water's edge, you'll arrive

at Lake Tear of the Clouds here, there, the highest water,
stewed brown by bark like stilled beer.
Those moments, out in the wild, when a man

confronts himself—the long, overgrown path
to the vision of arrival at one's own reflection—

you tried to line them up for all of us. If only
they could be put into words, right? Then, finally,

we could count them. It's not really a lake, Maurice,
but a col, a pool, the actual beginning
of the Hudson River, 4,000 feet up. There's a story

about Theodore Roosevelt trundling down
from its shores upon hearing death had pulled
its jangly carriage to McKinley's door,

the assassin's bullet behind his stomach
gangrenous at last. That's where Teddy learned

he was going to "take over the free world."
You'd know just how to care about something like that

even though the Iroquois name for Lake Tear was lost,
if ever it existed, and even though all those presidents

took the tribes apart like wolves
snapping wet ribs from an overrun chest.
You had such forgiveness. "I learn rivers

by sitting still," you said, and watched
your thousand selves
drift toward you and sail past—teacher,

poet, elder, runaway boy jumping the turnstile
for the A train—suspended amid silt
and coils of white birch, direct from the source.

The source, Maurice; a turtle
sunning on the rain-flattened lee of a fallen spruce

beside a lazy pond atop the Adirondacks.
Oh, we're all adrift on the shell of something.
We go to Brooklyn, Bayonne, Asheville,

New Orleans, Mexico, the Virgin Islands, and back
to guileless Saranac Lake, as though the trail

reached its summit and turned us, newly realized,
down the mountain again. Or how else

would we become answers? You were a secret

of the obvious, exactly like the country beneath
this country. The source, Maurice. When you find it—

when you step where the deer and bear, the Roosevelts,
the Iroquois stepped—you realize
it was never really hidden. The source hoots and bellows,

it stands at the podium, incanting
like a Mohawk emerged from beneath a tree line

to sing to the lake, to slide his glasses into their case,
to thank what can't be seen before receding
back to his shadowy offices among the brake.

VIEWING THE BODY BEFORE CREMATION

I thought I'd prepared myself
but when the blurry, hushed man told me
You can go in now,

I couldn't understand him.
The strings in the backs of my legs
had gone slack, my joints disconnected
like an unstrung marionette.
The visitation room

is right over there, he said. *Take
as long as you need.*
"Need." That's how he put it. His entire job

was to scuffle up and down
the carpeted hallways of the funeral home,
to remind the bereaved

there was something left to need. *I could
just sit here a minute,* I said. *Maybe.*
It was pleasant work, slow and indefinite.
A plastic chair floated beneath me,

the ground beneath that. No hurry,
I told myself. I could've rested there forever,

which would've been fine, which is why
the urn of coffee and the pamphlets
and the benches in the reception area

were put there: to consider forever.
That's just what I'll do, I told myself.
So I relaxed, leaned back, and watched
as I stood up to make my way down the hall.

PRAYER TO ENTER HEAVEN ALIVE, ONCE

Or just to peer between the elevator doors
like a nervous applicant, or from an observation deck
        somewhere in Tibet, to thumb a yuan into the slot,

spin the knob on the tower viewer and pick out
        an aloof, cloud-scudded sliver, gleaming high.
I have a lot of lasts waiting for me, God, and I need

        to sever my jealousy from its organ, to irradiate
and shrivel it before we meet. I can't be any part you.
        I'll have to stop loving one day, and then

a last breath, which predicates a last thought.
        How long will I have between those two?
I don't care about the meaning of life, or by which road

        pain drives its mule-cart into me, jangling
a curio shop upon metal hooks. What will be
        the last thing I forget? I held a flashlight in a tent

and swept away the night, but it kept coming back.
        The feel of that. If you told me the day,
I could stroll the pastures with an umbrella,

        ready for the right cyclone to deposit me close.
Or, no, sorry. Forgive the haywire powerplant I feed
        with dread below the dams, and its sparks,

its overflowed spillway jetting me to presume.
   I do not deserve to know the scent of the beyond,
be it oranges or burnt toast, or to wander near enough

   to hear its inverted bustle. Perhaps only
a postcard with a view of anything—a blind rectangle
   of white light—just to keep. Perhaps

a rub-on tattoo in the Cracker Jack, lord, or stick figures
   on a post-it above my bed, or maybe a final text:
a smiley, a thumbs-up. Not to confirm paradise

   but that there's a place, a way to see, manners
collected around a center. I pray there's nothing left
   to pray for up there, and no reason to come back.

II

SUSPECT

Now I remember how the policeman
asked me where I was
at the time of your death, and I thought
how nice of him to try
to cheer me up, joking that way
as the waves in his shoulder radio
crashed and whispered.
And then I listened to the frequency
of his lips and there wasn't a quiver,
not a single crest in the flatline
of his face and I knew he was seriously asking
whether I had killed my girlfriend.

If I had been a smarter man, a man
whose grip on the exposed wiring
of shock had not been so tight,
I would've seen it coming.
I would've inhaled and swallowed
the rotten, sulfuric taste of the entire
administrative holocaust to come:
papers exchanging hands
in distant offices, workers flitting
through the safety of their honeycomb,
their dirty feelers scraping our names,
and folders, finally, eating us whole.
"Why?" I asked instead,

knowing why, but wanting
to hear him say why. "We're just trying

to get all our ducks in a row," he said, "we
only want to understand."
Oh, officer, I never knew his name
but what a gift he was.
There was only so much understanding
to go around, and he wanted to drink
every drop of it, he wanted
to pound nails through the feet
of those ducks and drown them. "Home,"

I kept saying. Home, home, home.
He seemed to believe me,
which was funny because I knew
you were on the loose out there, fresh
as a cyclone crossing a prairie,
hovering, splitting and replicating, and
wherever I went or whatever I told him,
home had run away, dissolved, the way a word can,
the way a person can, the way facts and dates
and places end up blaming us, stupid us,
the ones who took the trouble to make them.

KEEPING APPEARANCES

Once in a while, someone will ask
how you died. I have no problem telling them,
even enjoy it a little,
the way the blunted syllables,
hung herself, roll
from the back of the mouth
out the front, finally struggling
to escape between lip and tooth.

Sometimes they'll ask *what*
was that like? and it's nice then,
like being asked to lead a dance
neither of us knows how to do.
First I nod my head, yes, then
I shake it slowly. No, no, no.

And sometimes, after that, they'll ask
what you were like, so perfectly.
Me knowing they're trying to help,
them knowing the labyrinth
of their emotions is empty now,
dark in the night of words. I am called
to study them who desire to hear
about a dead person they'll never meet.
They're good people, honestly, and then
I get to play the quiet game,

where I see how much of you I could forget
if I really tried. This is a little fun too

because I could be anybody, I can converse
with someone like me and pitch questions
then follow the breadcrumbs
out of the forest, back to the cottage of myself.
Isn't that fine? I could explain

that I'm not trying to shock myself. Or
maybe I am. Or maybe the one me knows
that the other me has a morbid fascination,
that hearing how I loved someone
who killed herself, specifically by hanging,
is instructive. Those people

are walking among us, and look
how naturally they act, how similar.
You'd have to lean in very close to hear
how many voices they're using,
to see the stitches and bolts
and how lovingly they've been put together.

THE EXCESS STAGES OF GRIEF

I'd pull up to the big intersection where Elm rams headlong
into crosstown four-lane traffic
and gape through the windshield. *I was going somewhere* I'd think,

the radio afroth, boiling love down to salt and tallow.
Those drives, I believed if I unfocused myself
things would mean more than their lines and shapes.
This must be depression, I'd sing, nodding, turning for the pet store

where they kept cats in furnished, glass apartments.
But there's that one stage where you start sweating at midnight

and don't stop until after sunrise, clutching the battery
from the overloud wall clock like a vial of antidote.
I'd been in it for a month or two. And before that

the one where you tell people you fucked the sad blonde
from the poolhall when really you couldn't get hard
and didn't even care. *What's wrong?* she'd asked, naked,
propped sideways on her elbow

so the streetlight through the shades couldn't wrap itself fully
around her hips. There's more to every naming
than even the spaces between the words. You could go to the doctor

like my ex did and they could say *we think you're making it up.*
She had seizures in Walmart, in the car, in the middle

of teaching a class, but the diagnoses kept curving her back
until she closed her own circle and had to be cut down
from the ceiling with a pair of scissors. More, care is a willingness
to chase the unknown into places where it shouldn't be,

to shout its name so the entire department store can hear
as you fling open the dress racks, riffle the innards of each freezer case.
Some people believe regret will give you cancer. Others,

that if you never love anyone you'll live forever, like opening the heart
lets tiny puffs of air inside, like the blood dries up in its course
toward desire. Now, five years away,

I buy the window seat for a flight and look down,
not ready to die at first, then growing slowly comfortable with the idea.
You won't even know, I tell myself, craning above the seatbacks

to see if anyone else's resignation is as utterly obvious
as mine. A woman clutches her baby—

who will die—cooing into its face, and a pair of lonely people
donut their necks and tug black masks over their eyes
and I ponder if, like me, they've accepted the futility of existence or

if there's a stoplight in them which simply blinks yellow
as though it's midnight in the small town of Self Preservation
and the traffic rests in its driveways, unthinking.
And am I still grieving, then, if I can't blink toward sleep

for even a second without wondering, calmly, *is this
what it will be like?* The wings slice through cumulus,

white tufts cling to the edges of the ailerons when, honestly,
I never imagined clouds could be harmed by anything manmade.

"TO ENRICH YOUR LIFE"

is the reason Steve tells me
we need to go see the latest theatrical abomination
as if my life's not rich enough,
as though the miniature treasure chest
in my ribcage is almost empty.
    What he doesn't know
is I sit up nights, by inkwell and candlelight,
counting the miserly fortune
of my regrets like God
budgeting the stars. And a few lovely comets

flouncing across a stage,
some sparkling banter, a musical number
can't compare to the grotesque
little putto who sits on my shoulder,
covered in ooze, blood dripping
from the raspberry of its nose.
    The good news is you're ugly enough
you won't have to worry about love again, it says
as I whack it a few more times
and a flurry of gold coins
sprays from the wounds like a celebration.

REHEARSAL

At Highwater Gallery,
a man in a bowler on a piano stool
sits before the alarmed mouth of a Revolutionary-era cannon,
blindfolded, waiting patiently for the fuse to burn down;

this, we learn, represents the sensation of sleep paralysis.
        "Bone chilling hallucinations and extreme terror,"
the photographer says, "to convey
conceptual meaning and mystery." Fine. But
it happened to me once, for real: the skiff

floated in gray water overhead and I flailed to surface,
to reattach my arms by stabbing at them
with emptied shoulders. Honestly, it was easy
to accept my body had been tossed overboard by sleep,
once I'd realized it. No "mystery":
the horror escaped in white streams of bubbles and I relaxed.
        To advance along the path
of enlightenment, certain Buddhist novices are locked

in a remote room of the ashram
and instructed to repeat "death, death, death" until
they visualize themselves as killers, as killed, as baby alive
a single moment, as baby a hundred years old
and doddering in hospice.
        The "preparation spectrum," maybe,
is what they should teach in school. We only witness
the rare artistic insight, such as Fuseli's *The Nightmare*,
with its obvious black mare at the foot of the bed,

a squat goblin on an aureoled woman's chest,
pinning her to languor; one doesn't feel she's dreaming
as much as stuck. If demons get bored,
they seem to enjoy sinking their claws into the line
between sleep and consciousness
and yanking hard, fucking with perception like it's a fire alarm.
           Morgue techs in South Africa, for example,

paused their morning paperwork mid-stroke
when a woman crumpled by a car accident the night before
coughed behind the refrigerator door. "Diagnosis of death
can fool you bad," the senior pathologist said;
personally, I melt at the romance

implicit in the word "diagnosis" here, the taxonomy and brow-
furrowed hemming of serious men who could, potentially,
diagnose a deceased person as something other
than dead. They study for years, they lay claim to terms

like "cadaver" and "catatonia," and yet they forget
to hold the mirror under the nostrils.
           Fiends and imps rolling,
laughing their asses off; "When we neglect precautions
against a fate so terrible, our tears are little less

than hypocrisy," writes Professor Wilder in 1896's
Premature Burial and How It May Be Prevented.
Inside my safety coffin, yanking the bell-line for escape,
I'd wonder instead upon what sinkhole-riddled purchase
my own definition of love was built. Who could I bury

without being absolutely certain they were gone?
　　　　Paint your own picture:
whosever face makes you beam moronic—spouse, whatever—
gone frantic, to-the-bone fingers scraping
the insides of their casket like a dog with a hock
on a hardwood floor. Is it your fault? Of course:
you could've leapt between the doctor and his pronouncement,
sobbing, or slapped the departed across the face

until they woke from whichever afterlife they'd tumbled into.
Post-cholera-era, a rash of exhumations preceded
a rash of communiques from beyond; not only nail-marks,
but stripped and half-digested clothes, greasy mummies

posed in curled, elbow-over-the-eyes resignation.
　　　　Held aloft for your own
1832 funeral procession on the shoulders
of the townsfolk in the English countryside, you'd cheer
when they rebelled against the church curate
who said—I swear to god—he "did not care"

about an oyster-woman's being stuffed in the ground alive.
They razed his house after that riot, on their way
to reducing churches, monasteries,
chapels to safe and healthy ash. They dug everyone up, just

to check. So much work, and that shink of spade
cutting through soil; I'm still in progress
toward covering my awe at those afflicted
who suspend chemo or respirator and claim

they're "ready to die," as though hypnotized

into acceptance by decades of reliable dreaming.
   I get it:
mis-parking, once, outside the funeral home and hurrying
through the wrong entrance, I stumbled upon the "casket
showroom." Glowing cases, wide-armed at the lid,

holding forth for an incontestable, grandmotherly embrace.
Totally empty, even of sound. Suddenly zonked,
drained, one has the urge to lie down inside a few.
   It won't be so bad,
you think, if you can just practice a few hours.

GEOCENTRICISM

Advice: to keep from lunging and caterwauling
while they're lowering your lover's coffin
    into the ground, momentarily imagine
Earth's revolution, which grinds at the precise speed

    to stand, to cry so tears fall instead of fly.
We could've been born to a planet
    where any child under ten pounds floats.
Or where day lasts week, and each week chars brittle

    as grilled skin over a drumstick. In point of fact,
six feet is a depth of surety, such that
    the particulates of plague couldn't erupt
through the London dirt. Epidemic prison, let's say,

    rain-fed, wafting skyward: the utter laziness
of the circling scavenger, inverted and shrunk.
    In the Adirondacks, the active layer of permafrost
runs near twenty feet deep and can burn out the gears

    from a backhoe mid-dig. And yet spouses die
in January, when it gets dark at four, when it's so
    viciously cold your eyes freeze if open too long
and you have to wait months, indoors, for death

    to be practical. "The Spindle of Necessity": that's how
Plato explained a tireless universe, stars and spheres
    whirling like whole notes on the rungs of a round staff.
He stared so hard up, the staring became a center.

The eyeglobe, the eyeworld, which asks why not
bend the alphabet, each number, every emptiness
        around itself? How do the blind even care about age?
Day was we'd lower pine boxes via rough-hewn rope,

        pulley, but it's vinyl straps now, a chrome automaton.
Spring, and the graves start growing like mushrooms
        and somewhere a morgue sighs itself empty.
It doesn't hurt so much to glance into the sky

        or even contemplate the crew of the Soyuz 11,
those Russian cosmonauts whose spirits drifted off
        at the rim of the thermosphere upon reentry.
The certainty out there, like gravity, so absolute

        that to casually suggest another theory of home
could liquid-nitrogen you to a blue-white rose. Or,
        empirically: here's terrible proof you'll survive longer
without sun than without home. I can't be certain

        of the soul, the notion, but there are times I'll stop
and steady myself against the wall and feel my sternum
        to check if I've cracked, that same startled way
a mother will drop her spoon in the soup

        when her daughter's car phone-poles like soft bread,
five states away. Such phenomena fill you heavy,
        submerge, so one stares through a layer
of translucent muck, seeking the horizon.

And the visible and invisible stars, Ptolemy claimed,
would appear and disappear in shifting orchestrations
        around a focus upon which we stand. Oh, that science!
I could reach down between its integers and variables

        and haul up a god, twenty gods, simple
as plucking wildflowers into a fistful of bouquet.
        It makes perfect sense when your head
is tilted forever back, squinting at points of light,

        to wear the heavens like a blanket on a winter night.
But gaze down from above without a body,
        then spin, slowly, to take in the vast reach.
Go on. Tell me what else there is to see.

        of the soul, the notion, but there are times I'll stop
and steady myself against the wall and feel my sternum
        to check if I've cracked, that same startled way
a mother will drop her spoon in the soup

        when her daughter's car phone-poles like soft bread,
five states away. Such phenomena fill you heavy,
        submerge, so one stares through a layer
of translucent muck, seeking the horizon.

        And the visible and invisible stars, Ptolemy claimed,
would appear and disappear in shifting orchestrations
        around a focus upon which we stand. Oh, that science!
I could reach down between its integers and variables

and haul up a god, twenty gods, simple
as plucking wildflowers into a fistful of bouquet.
    It makes perfect sense when your head
is tilted forever back, squinting at points of light,

    to wear the heavens like a blanket on a winter night.
But gaze down from above without a body,
    then spin, slowly, to take in the vast reach.
Go on. Tell me what else there is to see.

INSIDE THE WHALE

Almost like you've wanted to be eaten
your whole life, but eaten

not by something for sustenance,
no miasma of blood in dark water
nor teeth clinking bone,

but by accident, and by a cathedral,
and by a representative from
the infinite array of the unlikely.
So they could sing shanties of you

beneath the mizzen and mainsails,
and you, under the roof of a bandshell

made from ribs and salted steam,
could sing back—*Oh goodbye,
goodbye, cruel sand and sky*

and farewell forever to green—
wandering the tongue and guts
for some sign. No smoke,
no charred logs or bone spears

or colonies of fishermen afloat
on islands of kelp-lashed driftwood.
One must wonder what a thumb

tastes like. Or wait for waiting
until waiting throws you back and forth

like a clock on a clothesline.
Then, just when you're turning clear,
flaking away, a chance tickle
and you're sneezed free.
Isn't that how it always works?

You're nearly jelly and nothing matters
and then you're the bearded lunatic

stumbling the shoreline, one hand
cupped against your ear
like the echoes are only coming

from further away, like if only
the ground would move a little faster
you could catch everything
you ever wanted.

"IT'S CALLED GENERALIZED ANXIETY."

Awake I took the morning
to mean the world had
finally forgotten about me.
In the mirror I looked through
my eyes to find nothing wrong,
I mapped the curse of my face
on a palette shaped like a handprint.
There is no credibility to finding
a new season out the window, any season
and especially a wind that
throws the flowers into a panic.

I checked the phone to see if it was ringing.
I opened the door as a car
rushed over the pavement
towards a place where it would
inarguably stop. I stuck my finger
outside and it was like stirring
a bowl of warm water. How
anyone could ever tell
what temperature it was
is beyond me. And I had
a terrible feeling as I turned back—
it was like every thing was watching me
without caring and my breath
sucked up into the trees like newspaper,
never wanted to be in my chest. But

I had a terrible feeling just then
that the door wanted to swing free
circle itself and breathe and see
as I pushed it gently closed.

DISCOVERING AN APPARENTLY MISLAID COPY OF THE DIRECTORY OF THOSE WHO WILL BE LEFT BEHIND DURING THE RAPTURE

Thumbing through for your own name,
one notices first how the foredoomed
accrue around prolix labels:
"She Who Genuinely Desires Her Father,"

"Boy Who Ketchupped Cars from Overpass, #3,"
"Hit and Run of Pregnant Labrador." As samples,

these represent the softer, the morally thinkable;
there are bare hands on this planet
which dig for their pleasures through miles
of flesh. But skip the hideous,

let the gilded pages waft and flicker
like the silent ascension of a man from a wheelchair.
It's a beautiful object. This catalog might be

the last beautiful object, which is why
it makes you cry. Maybe, you think,

maybe if I can remember the worst thing
I ever did,
maybe if I ask my mother. Maybe if I love my mother.
But no—the clear water of this code, your whole life,

and you of yellow oil. You, who stopped deciphering
long ago, content with pinched orgasms, with throwing

the Thanksgiving leftovers away,
you who worshipped your nerve endings instead, and for that
you might suffer. Might. One pitchfork

through the liver, another the throat,
perhaps an overcoat of spumous flame: does pain hurt
if you know, beyond any doubt, it doesn't equate
to death? You could be the doorman,

the courteous one who opens the gate
and welcomes them up from below
with outstretched hand. How about that?
Buy a little hat, a uniform.

Come right in, you'll say. *I'm here
to help.* I bet the damned recall
courtesy fondly and appreciate ambassadors. I bet

they'll even let you yarn the lever-wheel on the rack,
even hacksaw through the femur

of a demented maniac: you'll be of use.
The future narrowed, emptier, yet spacious for we
who keep our heads.
And if it gets tough, just keep droning,

like a monk in mantra,
this isn't hell. There is no hell. This is the plan.

BADMOUTHING
THE RECENTLY DECEASED

Toeing gravel at the mouth of the drive,
we snort, hide our laughter from the house;

the windows have a babysitter's blank stare.
"Worthless bastard never once
returned an email. Could've sent him the cure

and he would've missed it."
It's hot. The cicadas throb a low electric hum
carved out from the dusk and we're drifting,
drifting beyond ceremony's rocky grip,

beer cans clutched and dripping.
We remove our suits one article at a time
like children after church, like if we confess

how real we are—saggy arms, stained t-shirts,
hammocks of sweat at the pits—

we'll age in reverse, before we were marching
in this god-awful procession. Long past

the rhetoric of neat humanity, when
we had to preface each declaration with, "He
was a good guy, but…," we bludgeon
his stupid jokes, his ear-hair, that open sewer:

his breath. I'd say we were ruthless
except the deceased is suspended midair
just above, laughing right along

that way we dream of giggling at ourselves,
relieved of pride at last: a mother
spanks her son in public. A daughter

wipes her father's backside. But we
correct our imbalance
by circling an emptied space, smashing a fist
flat into its frozen smile until it's gone.

PHONE CALL TO PLAN ABORTION, AS FLOOD

She says she's lost so much weight
since our break-up that she can see it,
she can feel her hips spreading out
as though her womb were a river
and the water was rising around
a lump of clay caught in its path.
She can't keep from crying. She tries,

knowing how hard it is for me to hear,
but her levies are broke and gone:
waterlogged-teddy-bear gone,
family-photo-album gone, gone
as the christening gown blown
into a tree two towns away, gone. She says

in Texas, now, they make you listen
to the heartbeat. They take your ultrasound
and show it to you and make you hear
the twice-quickened rhythm against
the backdrop of yourself. She says

what hurts most is that it's a piece
of me she's losing, the last piece, and if
there was any part of me that wanted
to pull from the wreckage this family,
I should do something. I should do

something, but I can't. If you need
any help, I say, let me know. If you need
any, any help, anything at all, I'm here.
I am so artful in my evil, it takes
three of me to keep myself
from running back into the house
and lying down on the linoleum
to wait for her to swallow me alive.
Okay, she says. Okay. It's like searching

for bodies. Out there, somewhere,
the ragged corpse of goodbye
is waiting for us to find it, but instead
we stay on the line, petrified
that when we hang up it will be the last time
we'll ever hear each other breathe.

POEM FOR THOSE BORED
BY PERPETUAL TRAVESTY

At a certain point, nothing is you.
You're not the student when the shooter bursts in
nor the mother with a bomb sewn

into her womb, nor the businessman bouncing
in the malfunctioned plane. If you were,
you'd know it by now. Your soul

would be pounding the metal walls as the ship
goes down, your screams would be caught
in a wayward air pocket in the engine room.

But only you are you, sitting down to stare
at the nightly news or check the scores
on your phone. You know how to stash yourself away,

to fold up humanity and slide it under the couch,
into the overhead bin. We pray, of course,
for less pain. But, oh, how we protect ourselves,

how my excess must trump your need. We pray
to pray enough to secure our end, to reach up
and find the hooks and harness dangling. We pray

the angels cry instead, whose mouths
never feed. Those angels never make a peep, so we pray
to put them to use by heaping our weight atop

their radiant heads. Or maybe, just once, they might
     explain what it's like to observe from on high
and cure us this incessant yearning to find out.

III

GASOLINE WAS A TRIGGER

Then there were the times
we'd pull up to the Valero
but forget to roll up the windows
or we'd do it too slowly or
the dense, flowerless odor would creep
through the pinioned ductwork
in the undercarriage of the car
and you'd try smiling, you'd try to finish

your point about how a word
means what it feels like, about how cocoon
was such a great word since it wraps
around itself and seems to emerge
with some honest meaning, perhaps
brilliant, masterful in its nearly revolting
sonic quality—the wet, doubled velars giving way
to the long, soothing ease of the open glottis—

but by then the smell would've gotten you,
triggering some mechanism
buried beneath consciousness, nerves giving up,
your head twitching and muscles
taut as the hull of a submarine
and you'd begin the slow descent into seizure
where all you could do was hatch a rictus grin
and choke out small sounds, "oock…chrohmm…"
sweet, really, trying to keep me from worrying
or jamming my foot on the pedal
in an attempt to spirit us to the ER,
which you hated. So I'd pump the gas

        as you writhed and mortised in the seat,
and we'd drive home in silence,
and then I'd pull the furniture of your body from the car
and carry it up the stairs
and lay you on the living room floor. I'd ball up
your coat and put it under your head,
then feed the animals to keep them
from stomping and grinding you into the carpet.
You had meant to educate me, yet again,

        on how certain thinkers believe language
a graveyard and the sense we make
is merely the reading of the names of the dead
from their tombstones. We'd grown accustomed
to suspended lessons, interrupted so often
by paralysis and fear that we learned the timing,
how to repeat ourselves, how to denote
rather than connote; you painted half-finished portraits
of critical theory, and I interpreted
until I could go no further. Then you'd explain,

        over and over, the transistors
within human energy, how belief in love and connection
negated the philosophical conjurings of linguists,
and placing the word where it needed to be
perfected the notion of communication
to the point that theories couldn't touch it,
to where it would fire and explode
and emerge from the wreckage of intellectualism
in awesome singularity, hovering above,

leaking in, emanating like an aureole,
like the corona of the human mind
stilled at the center of some sickness,
combusting, a machine lurching forward
in an attempt to escape from itself.

BLISS

We laid down to pull, one by one,
the strings in each other's bodies.
I raised your legs,

poured nakedness out
the wheelbarrow of your jeans,
then ran a palm across

your thighs' brown acreage
and you explained, "I used to do it

to wake myself up." Towlines of thick blades
were imprinted, shining in your flesh, almost
like an animal had wandered underneath

and was clawing at the bark of your skin
from the inside. "Why?" I whispered,
kissing the firm, upturned lip
of each and every scar.

If all you ever did was breathe
and every breath was a moan
like the one you let escape as I moved inward,

I never would have sought an answer.
We could still be in bed this minute,
growing so large we could touch
every corner of each other at once.

But you wanted more
or you knew that this was it or, you told me,
because something is inside that steals
from the garden of your consciousness
and must be excavated and destroyed.

I reached in and plucked
the heavy fruits that came free with a sigh,
I tugged at the silver stems
of the small infinity we tended,
but I could never understand. "Just

don't do it again," I said. You smiled
because you couldn't promise,
because at that moment the razor

was so sharp it trimmed me away from you,
who I could never be, who had mined a sunlight
so permanent and terrible it would be hard
to swear, merely for love,
that you'd never dig for it again.

ONLY HERE FOR SUPPORT, I STRUGGLE TO RESTRAIN MYSELF FROM OFFERING ADVICE TO THE BEGINNING PALLBEARER

One thing though: don't breathe. Show respect.
Huff along quietly, white-lipped,

brass handles and lugs steamed warm
against your palm. Use two hands. Watch your step.
Mostly, your manner will be automatic

like whispering in the museum.
Nobody warns you, nobody could warn you
how little this arrangement weighs

but you'll forget immediately anyway, sliding
the whole parcel into the hearse
like a hand into a black glove.
          Now every moving piece of your body

is a symbol: the heel and toe, the stress inside the neck,
the bread and meat from breakfast wending their way

through your bowels. My first,
they asked me five minutes before. I told myself,
You're going to lift your dead grandmother
in the air now. It helped

to peel reality from its frictionless backing;
the spark that ignited the cosmos
with incandescent feeling
didn't live inside that box. That box a black hole

and you just the astronaut crawling a safety rail
back to the bay doors. Of the unbelievable machine,
you're the inept repairman. That's all.
Morticians will hire certain solemn-looking boys,

big boys in navy suits who sing at Sunday mass
to carry anyone they're asked.
            Don't ask anyone

how they knew the deceased. Held aloft,
you know them as the Earth knew them, moving slowly
beneath the gyroscope that kept head above feet
as long as it could. I'm not saying you're gravity,

but, rather, that comparing familiarities
paints you selfish under the burden of burden,
that you never knew what dignity meant
until this moment. You don't want to be tall.

You don't want to be the one reaching way up, either,
like one kid pushing another up a wall; it's a team effort.
You and me, we won the blessing inside unremarkability.
The giants die young and never die, the petite

exhale rarity like beauty but we, the average,
            we carry each other together,

ants toward the mound,
posts stretching far into some infinite plane
where the fence hardly seems to matter.

IF YOU END BENEATH
THE BIG GRAVE ON THE HILL

Whatever you do, don't lord it over the others,
the lawn-levels, the flushes, the pillow markers.
If you're marble, don't intimate the richness
in your veins. Be granite of spirit, igneous,

plain and forgiving as an unopened book.
Like a fat god, you'll never have to move.
Your acolytes will arrive with tribute: bouquets,

lanterns, stacks of coins spread out like a golden quilt.
With time, you'll learn how to decipher
what each of these people need

by how light catches in the wet soffits
of their eyes. They come to gaze into your face

and dream, their emptied passenger seats
and wedding tables and rocking chairs
filled with whatever magic you can muster. Tempting

to tell them some green and hopeful lie, but shut up.
Recall that right after *Love is patient, love is kind,*
the scripture promises *where there are tongues,*
they will be stilled. Nobody remembers,

so they'll speak to you as lunatics to a brick wall.
Be still. Be kind. They want a sliver of a star
to be secreted inside you, something that sings

when it shines. Let them believe. And don't heed
the white screams of crows. Don't crumble.
Don't forfeit your meaning when a belt of moss

tickles the tethers of your waist. You have
only two jobs: to stand, and to not fall down. No,

they're not the same. One you do for yourself,
the other you do for the person inscribed
in your chest. Yet be aware you may
never know what you say. A graveyard

is a city of reflection without mirrors.
But if you're really lucky, one day

a curious child might come to take you away
rubbed on a sheet of rice paper with black coal.

WHERE IT RAINS OTHER THAN RAIN

A featherlight drizzle of spiders in Australia,
for example, which precipitates certain locals
lowering themselves from bridges and fortified over-
passes on intricate riggings of high-tensile fishing line:
not because they believe arachnids gods,

but for fear the one god might rapture via filament
the most fervent. Of course, the language of the holy
is symbol, which mortals strain to speak.
What to make, then, of a coastal nowhere in India

that sees blood storms once a decade?
Grocers, deliverymen screaming in the streets,
mundus stained as though they'd waded
a river of cherry wine. One young couple
whose wedding appears as a survivor's count

from a bus accident. Out there, the shivering devout
will kneel, recite scripture, band together at the sites
where a loud someone claims to have hovered
or necromanced or hacked down a redwood
with a single stroke. There's an entire economy

for supply and demand of deity, like blood pudding,
liver and onions, the insides offered to the outside,
offered in again. We, as a particular genus of soul,
represent one for another to the extraordinary
as blind feathers hoping to unfold to a peacock.

In homey Louisiana, they get downpours of fish
and worms, on a certain day in Oregon a mother
could leave the morning cereal in its bowls
on the back porch for a deluge of milk. The incredible
occurs once, or twice, or freshwater minnows

fall annually from the heavens above Yoro, Honduras;
it's no matter. The divine operates through precedent.
One jogger circling one pond in one dusk, struck
by lightning despite a complete lack of clouds.
It will happen again, an arc unfurling from the clear,

orange horizon to rip us from our running shoes.
And since study loves repetition,
scientists soon arrange to listen at the chests
of such anomalies, to locate and wheedle and square
the un- with the natural: it's a spore from a lake,

it's sediment, it's a migratory phenomenon
and each pelican opens its mouth
at the exact same instant. But if the strange
means anything, then its explanation
means less. The Greeks adhered

to emission theory, how the eyes beam light
out and back like we each operate
a TV studio inside our heads. This was always
the original dream: to create and record
and watch the self in action, to loop

the laugh track when sight radiates a dog
chasing its tail. To be in front and behind,
that's it. To punch in at the offices of the interstitial
and stroll home with an umbrella after work,
palms up, checking the sky for what comes next.

"MORE GRATEFUL THAN EVER"
NBC News *Headline*

The thigh scar rounds an empty shell
where muscle heaves silently upward

like a deepwater wave: you have to look at the photo
of the shark attack survivor
a good thirty seconds

before it stops being ugly. And then yes: who cares what
keeps us from turning inside out.
In my car one night, I asked a girl, "You ever stare into a mirror

until all you see
are shapes?" I was lurching toward the bravado
required to kiss a stranger,

sidling up to it
as though preparing to lunge and swallow.
"That's dumb," she said, giving me instead
the drawn curtain of her hair

as she turned to stare at streaks of rain on her window.
Jagged ridges
atop a red seam; they say in terror—real,
horror movie terror—

you can't even tell you're screaming. It's just noise,
autonomic. You're the doll in the toddler's hand,

you're thrashing against the unknown, trying to stuff
your stringy guts back inside in your belly. I started the car.
I drove,

two hands against the clock's green light.
Oh, such finality!
Its skin shined

in the streetlights
with a burn victim's painless sheen. What time will you have
for life
to flash before your eyes? I don't recall

dropping her off, or what was offered in goodbye.
I thought hard about how
she'd never think of me again.
The quiet in the car after, though,

and the space
where longing collected
to reach up and shake me by the stomach

before receding to its black depths, down
where blood
tastes exactly like the air you breathe.

PROJECTION

Now I have conversations with you
I couldn't when you were alive.
I lie down on the living room carpet

and you ask me "Do you think
I'm too sick to love? Am I
not worth it anymore?" In the sunlight

the angels of dust fall
when I think about God and,
if he exists, how surprised he must be
when nobody cares what he wants.
The look on his face. Maybe

it even hurts him, that sudden
updraft of pain under the stomach
when the hidden center of joy
is ripped out and thrown into the open.

Never, never, I say.
"But I can't walk. Some days
I can't speak. How can you love me?"
The size of people:

I rub my cheek on the blue fabric
and whatever observes us—

I can feel it—claws at its invisible floor
to get through, to down here
where love asks itself why it exists.
Because I want to,

I say, gripping tightly to the ground
as though waiting to be plucked away.

VARIATIONS ON TROUBLE

Of course, this is language's fault,
or the fault of everyone who ever taught anyone
to use it inaccurately, or knowing that it is
inaccurate, using it anyway. How to define

my aunt, for example, recovering from cancer
in Albany when her treatment uncoiled inside her
and struck her dead like a blown spring.
This is *tragedy*, because it is also

irony. Or, receiving a phone call
from my girlfriend's ex-husband late at night
to hear that she leapt from the Earth
on the end of a short rope: this is for me,

my own sharp inheritance of time
called *crisis*. It is also *disaster*, as in the crumbling
of one world to reveal a molten sadness beneath.
The fortress of days that build themselves

so high I can't see their steeples: this is *calamity*, *woe*,
distress. And then others arrive, literal agents
of death: policeman, doctor, coroner, grief
counselor, undertaker, incinerator, all of whom

see this as *dilemma*. This is the modern term
for what we've got, as in modern war, how
the living are burned along with the dead. Departing
from form into mass, from material into immaterial

like sand into glass; this is *misfortune*. The witnessing
of heartache within your own chest: this is *pain*
which, as everyone knows, is too simple a concept
to need a word. Always this flatness of speech,

crisp at its edges and trampled underfoot
before it's ground into the cold surface of fate.
This is *trouble*: people gathered together to speak
to a cake of earth on the eve of something new,

people falling silent. People alone in their houses
with a feeling that there's something they've learned,
something so big it empties the room and nobody,
nobody able to find the words to talk about it.

THEORETICALLY, I'M BOTH
DEAD AND UNBORN

More fascinating than the gravity or the rank breeze
or the sensory-verified New York street
is the sound waiting beneath the piano
suspended over the sidewalk, the way chaos *could*
circumvent the beauty perched atop its keys. And the movers

against the red brick, smoking, perusing the women
who stroll past; in this picture it's wonderfully unclear
why work has been paused, or against the forces of nature
which direction we're engaged in rooting for. Yet some
magnetic pole urges interaction—I'd be thrilled

to stand beneath this teetering megalith a minute, cross-armed
as though the creak overhead, the ping of the rope, the puddle
of shadow oscillating around my feet didn't matter a tick:
ceci n'est pas une mort imminente. Or at least, conversely,
it's the demonstration of comfort inside a multiverse

where one bellicose me dares things to go wrong.
James Dean me. Lady Godiva me. Quantum physicist me
does this experiment where he presses a thick finger
down upon time's clicking turntable, discovers a black hole,
and then drops a single person in, just to hypothesize who

will be dragged in behind and why, like love
was the human chain and we're all those links following
darkness to the bottom (though there is no bottom): you need
a patient zero in order to successfully destroy humanity.
Call him Regular Joe. Amazing Joe. Colin Scott, even,

who wandered off the trail in Yellowstone and fell
in 200-degree acid springs while his sister looked on.
They searched, but he'd boiled away, dissolved, like some 22
anti-pathic, touristic rebels before him. In the TV film version,
during the ranger's admission they'd ceased the rescue,

that's when the strings would come in, the orchestra.
Imagine the songsmith with blank sheet on the music rack,
composing for "Hiking to Lake Disaster: A Lifetime Original."
The bulk swings overhead, almost frivolous in its apathy
of how stupid, how fat-renderingly worthless we are

without the sorcery of each other. Prabu Bhatara, Nabarangpur,
India: on his way back from a wedding, he stumbled upon
an injured bear and tried to snap a quick selfie. About him,
I don't care. But the stray dog who attempted a snarling,
Davidic rescue—the *stray* dog, like some deity fired

such canines aimlessly across the land—I'm relieved to read
it survived and went on straying. There, too, I wish
I could offer bear and dog a home, bathe and groom,
soothe myself when they wandered off together,
not to return for days. A note plucked to reverberate

in a frequency no one has ever heard before,
that's the real experiment, like emptying the pool expressly
so an ignoramus on his phone might fall in, headfirst,
or not headfirst but broken and sobbing at the 3-day growl
his starvation threatens, or drowned in four inches of a green,

algal remainder, or each misfortune simultaneously.
Not Freud's death drive, not Saint Paul's blathered, amateurish
cupio dissolvi—like a spell to evaporate inside the stomach
of the afterlife—nor any other wish to leave corporality
for higher ground, but the opposite as defined by a fixed point

we could call "complete stillness." This represents the lone,
necessary impossibility inside our laws. Ultimately, the movers
must go back to work, must hand-over-hand drag the machine
where it can't hurt. Wires on a wire, really, taut as a promise
one makes while grimacing up at the everchanging heavens.

WHATEVER NATURE MEANS

One of your bad days. I was doing
anything to keep you from crumpling
to the floor, from seizing
and convulsing. I said, to massage your mind
against your illness, "Why do you love

nature?" Not two days earlier,
I'd seen you hold a wasp in your palm
and carry it from the living room
to the front door, a black jewel
buzzing its way back to the earth.
You'd rescued squirrels, pulled a duckling

from the maw of a snapping turtle,
splashing your way into the cold water
like a mother panicked in the dark.
"I don't love nature," you mumbled.

"No?" I said, running my hands
up and down your sides. "Then why
do you try so hard to save it?"
You snorted, a laugh knocking its way
down your hallways, collapsing.
"I've never saved anything," you said.
There was a time when I

was taught not to play with wild animals,
when someone explained rabies and venom
and the utter silence inside the stomachs

of beasts. I wanted to ask you who
said it was okay to touch nature that way,

what day passed differently
that pried the jaws of fear from around you,
but it was too late. The coils of a seizure
constricted your ribs, your neck.
Your teeth clenched as you hit the carpet

and I followed you down, pressing you,
holding on until you were out of danger,
feeling your body's incredible need
and the nothing I could give you against it.

ARGUMENT FOR THE DESPERATION
MANIFEST IN WORSHIPPING SNAKES

One can comprehend the appeal

of pulling a warm velvet rope
to ring down the divine.
Or in the service of desire,

submitting to the adrenal tug o' war:
a music maker tied to one end
and at the other, leaping

between two pearlescent electrodes:
eternal silence.

You can inject the heart
with such excitement,
transform it from a lax,

timeworn cavern
into a church longhouse,
parishioners ecstatic with song,
stomping the dusty floorboards.

Nothing escapes ecstasy,
not a stitch of sweat-soaked flannel
nor the hammer-light dulled

in the bronze topographies
of belt buckles and jean buttons,
all caught inside believing as a barn

wandering a whirlwind.
Be here, the air commands.
Find. Release your terror like a knot

plucked open by a smooth yank.
Locked inside the tongue

there is a language beyond death
and a body need only raise the meat
of its hands to the rafters, gaze up,

and like a syringe into a vein
slip into that conversation
with the numinous, the perpetual dialog

between us mice scratching in the walls
and the hot mouth which promises
never to consume us.

CHANGE

Past dark, a clattering like hooves
stamps and pounds at the neighbor's door.
"I swear to God I'll kill myself!" the man vows.
He sobs.
The neighborhood hides behind a newspaper.

I nod—yes. Yes: that's how I've made my covenants,
too: whipping and spurring, trained on the horizon.
Midway across the overpass to school,

I grabbed a girl once, hard between my hands
when she told me we were done.

"Let go!" she screamed.
Autonomically,
I sunk my talons into her shoulders. "I can't!"
The cars whooshed below, straining to hear

as she wrenched away. Control
is an illusion, the attributionists warn, they

who inspect mental patients through glass walls.
As in, no choosing can matter. A faint tinkling

in the night and I cock my head: it's a xylophone
of coins against a wooden deck,
sprung loose while rummaging his pocket.
He's out there still, digging for his phone,

for something to whisper at. Or maybe
it's simply his reward, a treasure spread at his feet

for believing enough in the divine to give
rather than take: "I swear to God!"
No, wait,

I know this sound: he's turned himself
completely inside out. Next,

he'll gape down in disbelief
at whatever it is he's actually worth.

DOGGY HEAVEN

Full of all the cats
that went to cat hell
and long strings of raw sausage
dangling from the windows
of empty storefronts:
it's a festival of disobedience.

All the rows of ten-penny teeth
gleaming in the forever sunshine,
latching onto slow and ghostly bumpers.
All the dry tongues and wet noses,
the ambiguous canine smiles
all relaxed and happy, going a little crazy
in the afterlife. Having earned it.
Having to us been
the faithful symbol of our character,
an accessory of all men

who go to our own heavens
only to find those homey, baleful eyes
nowhere in sight. Truly

the saddest thing is that they separate us.
That given the gift of love and companionship
we soldier through our lives feeling heroic

turning back to see them following, and then
at the end, nothing

but an unanchored line of people
that goes on forever.

IV

POEM IN PREPARATION
FOR MY LAST WORDS

To come bubbling from some deep reserve,
come knocking down the hallway from the white light
    like a tooth from an upturned drainpipe
while I lie in that last bed, studying that last ceiling.
    I loved, I chased a camel made of green money

across each desert laid before me. With my mouth,
    I could very nearly replicate the snapping sound
of a new book's spine. I've learned. I've provided.
    In that moment, I've heard how some souls recall
a nursery rhyme in another language—*dormez-vous!*—

    and still others the promising to a lover
they would bring Malbec instead of Merlot.
    Some say nothing, but the crabgrass
tickles their necks after the picnic, or they sniffle
    when a chemical nudge ignites a wilted synapse

and their first puppy's muzzle warms their tired palm.
    In that exhaustion, I wish the wakeful nerves
and the effusive nerves strung together as an open,
    untouched staircase in the burning building
of the body. Let me mean something. I'm begging,

    even unto the breath I escape from, even unto
that long line I've drawn as though dragging a pencil
    behind me since birth, pressed to the ground,
accruing length away from stupidity: god of punctuation,
    before you measure and spool, I pray for period.

HUMAN CHAIN

"Don't worry" I say to my friend
as he's lolling on the hospital's starch-white pillow
after an obvious interior shattering
at the conference keynote reading. They'd escorted him,
scarlet and hyperventilating, up the aisles
from the auditorium's front row
in such a way that any empathic person
must have surely sunk into a fuller cognizance
at the fragility of the human mind
upon simply glancing into his strained, tear-streaked face.
How ethereally we've been constructed: Frankenstein's
monster, for instance,

was stitched not from scraps of bodies, but foremost
from Frankenstein's wispy ideas. Yet then
there's those tender moments in the story
when this goliath—built purely from curiosity
and arrogance—really, actually, learns to read;
he may as well have picked up bone saw and scalpel
and mashed an extra set of brains into his own skull.
Later that night,

I entered the wrong dormitory and startled
an absolute stranger who, up until that moment,
lived in a halcyon surety that no midnight beasties
or fang-silhouetted creepers would trespass the arbors
of sleep. This is true: the architects of such complexes
design them without any marked complexity,
and my shadow looming in the bedroom door

must've appeared a nightmare made flesh. "Don't
worry:" it's quite possibly the stupidest,
the most inside-out command

ever uttered, and yet we touch the hems
of each other's arms, tenderly, and repeat it like magpies
atop a split-rail fence. "If you tell someone
they're breathing," a child explained one Thanksgiving,
"they'll think about breathing and breathe different";
that same old story of thought
fighting action, the autonomic pleading to be automatic.
In 1949, the lobotomy

was posited using an ice-pick-esque surgical instrument
inserted into the space above the eye, through the socket,
to jibble the patient's emotions into focus, like stirring
a stew to an exact thickness; the procedure
won a Nobel Prize. This is also true:
we celebrate these attempts to treat intellect as if
it were a television with a cycling screen
and simply required delicate tuning and a tightening
of a few, integral screws. Trepanned cranial plates, too,
can be dated

to 7,000 years before Christ, and certain early doctors
would open their patients like jewelry boxes and drop one
or two leeches in, to "soak up the sadness-causing excess
of bile." The police came, separately,
for both me and my friend. They gave me the task
of proving the unprovable; that my criminal entry
was an honest mistake, that I wasn't a creature wheeling

through the darkness to hover over the precipice of terror.
He—friend—simply explained how something
pulled him under and he needed help until it let him go.
Supposedly,

the mummified arm of such a lake monster resides
in a Tokyo Buddhist temple; the "kappa," it's called,
yanked travelers, fishermen, even sploshing bathers under
unless they bowed first before entering the water.
That's what garnered blame for drownings:
a lack of manners. I'm reminded of those
midwestern communities who'd lock arms when a child
disappeared at the beach, and walked together
into the shallow tides to seek a tiny, rock-trapped,
claspingleaf-weed covered corpse. Don't worry, don't worry,
don't worry: before they

took him away my friend began repeating his own name
as though it were wriggling to escape the cocoon
of his head and make its own life amid the million tons
of suffocating, ludicrous thoughts swirling above
the reading, sprung free by art. Some nights,
we need to be invaded. Others, the dusky walls
of the bedchamber need to crumble away until we're
ruthlessly united, calling en masse, answering
through the black like flashlights announcing
a search party among the corridors of a crowded,
dumbstruck wilderness.

POEM IN CASE WE BECOME SOLDIERS

I've begun practicing with a shade of red called "lust."
I paint red stars on my sneakers, the coffee table,
on the envelopes I mail to Time Warner. Lust

is militant in the sense it's beyond moderation,
as when the weak lion risks his life

to corral a female into thicket. See how
that type of desire wears a uniform,

see how one can watch it dominate
like a policeman at a daycare center?
After a time, my living room walls

resemble a night bleeding from its beginnings.
But being American

dulls one to the shock of duplication,
one idea built on the wreckage of another, like limbs

piled on a battlefield. Stars and stars and stars, and
a game to see who can draw the best, free-hand.
Then a game to see

what we can "do without": fresh fruit, Google,
time of day, wanting, wanting to be wanted.
Finally, I stand against the wall, spread-eagle,

my five points splayed
as though I were part of something larger. No,

as though something larger were coming
and my stomach, my soft parts
had been cured their foolish longing

for the blink of instinct,
that posture whereby the palms point face-out
as a creature denying the inevitability of pain.

ELEGY FOR THE DRIVE-IN

I used to like how the heads
were so big they were the size of Buicks
and how the picture jumped on breezy nights
like a hand
feeling under a blanket

and how the tension of the part
when the two young rebels
decided to play chicken
reached inside and made you
for a moment actually believe in youth
how you could feel everyone else

believing and reaching there
towards the blank history
that didn't give a damn
and was growing farther and farther away
like a flat stone skipping
towards the bottom of a pond

and knowing that inside the little
boxes of cars were thrumming hearts
that pounded like naked fists
on midnight doors and driving
quietly into the distance after

how your smallness came back into you
how you were warm with possession
from this that you could never hold

and the smell of exhaust in your hands
wild and sad as it dispersed
like the emptiness the waterhole feels

when the animals leave it for the sun
and I miss knowing that it was there
for my nights and then knowing
it was there for everyone who so wantonly
jailed inside their cars watched the world
with so many new kinds of love

I TOOK THAT LANDSCAPE
FROM YOUR BATHROOM

Also, a sack of scarves, a decorative lamp shaped like a star,

and a miniature poodle who displays
literally no compassion towards people, who won't lick
or fawn or spring into your lap

while you're sitting on the toilet at 5am
sobbing uncontrollably at a painting
of which there must be 500,000 reproductions
keeping watch like hidden cameras

over the lavatories of the universe.
I hung it where you hung it, this idea

of countryside. It's lovely;
it's almost enough to make a person forget
that nature doesn't give a shit about anything,

not slavery or Nazis or stockbrokers
tossing themselves from the signposts of industry
to land on a sheath of pavement below

and certainly it didn't care about your fragile,
overburdened body, full of pain and terrible intention
as you scaled the porch railing that night,
tied the noose, and made no plans

to ever touch the ground again. One wants to believe
in the sympathy of nature, how it dreams
of lush grass that never needs rain, zebra

sharing blueberries with lions, a lake
of peppermint tea. But nature is a god

who doesn't share. It hardens and stares,

an ancient, mustachioed face behind glass
swaying a bit on its bracket of rope
in the unbelievable breeze it makes, like a joke.

IMPASTO

I arrived before makeup and haircut,
before they massaged the bruises away
or even latched the eyelids shut, so
I could almost divine in her dried, corneal glass

the distant horizon she escaped toward, like the dust
kicked up from black hoofbeats
hung yet over a darkening plain; I took a picture

because I didn't know what else to do.
This was in the "slumber room,"
after the morticians slid their latex hands
across her landscape;
          I took a picture
because I didn't know what else to do.

Someone had tucked her up to the chin
          with a red blanket, like a red satire of sleep.
Her forehead cold against my lips;

          I didn't need to know how it felt
until after the feeling was inside me, kissing
a wall between howl and silence and then

I didn't need to know.
High on the observation deck,
          you press against skyscraper window
to wonder down at whoever looks like ants.
But then all that matters

is the cold against your skin. Like that:
you couldn't delete her picture either, for fear
of not knowing what spectacle to commemorate.
       Or how about I visited home one year
and from between the pages

of some children's book, a crimson maple leaf
fluttered to the carpet like a great, peeled scab.
It came from a day I desperately wanted
       to tattoo, to remember
yet didn't, and instead I found secreted

in that shrunken bedroom the memory
       of the person who deposited himself
inside symbol.
Be careful what you think, I thought to myself.
Nobody tells you the way to see the beloved dead;

you look, and your mourning withers and falls
and all you want is a relic of the belief

that there are no wrong answers when it comes
       to relinquishing love.
After the atomic bomb
sears shadows into the wooden siding of the barn,

you don't scrub them away. And you couldn't
delete her picture either, even stumbling upon it
       years later, among a folder of images

from your niece's ballet recital.
    I was hunting a series of moments
that equaled one another, that didn't drain time

to a white-knuckled choke. I've tried to erase
that last picture. But I want to know what it's like

to be all of me remembered. That red blanket and—
    I promise—a little grin she meant me to keep.

I GUESS I KNEW SHE DIDN'T CARE ANYMORE WHEN SHE STOPPED WASHING HER FRUIT

which isn't fearlessness, but a subtler pantomime
figuring depression, which means whatever poison

they belch onto the groves or orchards or crops
can't matter to her organs, which means "here,
go on and erase these 45 seconds

of my life, I don't need them."
Like sliding a wedding ring into the center
of a poker table. For how long
after dispassion toward sustenance

follows fatal apathy, drifting down the sluice
of the Leprosy spectrum, into
the clefts and cordons of the flesh,

then brain, then heart?
What would you do if someone you loved

was visiting, say, the Grand Canyon
and took one step closer the rim
than you wanted? Then detached and threw
one whole leg in? I wish it didn't—I really gaze up
and pray to a god I don't know
I believe in—that this wasn't because

I've been eaten by depressed people in the past,
sometimes rind first, sometimes in one
hot chomp. Haven't you? Isn't it exactly how

you'd imagine being swallowed by a whale
or tiger or black-tongued Moloch?
What's horrifying

is you can't even blame them—
those poor depressives—it's how they were born,
and how you were born, too, you normie,
        you sterling little creature of god,

you who witness sadness as deformed beauty,
which is the best kind. The baby screams,

the three-legged dog chases its own smile
and your heart bumbles from one rainstorm
        to the next, gazing down into each puddle
with that quizzical, cock-headed stare,
as though wondering whose tears could be so big
and whether they feel cleansed to be rid of them.

EXTRACT

I can't tell if it was the admixture
of all the fragrances—Obsession, Je Reviens,

Shalimar, Lucky You—or one in particular
that brought you into coalescence
as I was passing between ladies' shoes
and the wall of Snuggies
at the off-price department store. I closed my eyes,

tilted my head back, and wandered,
arms out straight as a pair of dowsing rods,
divining with all my might. That one night
I waited on the couch for twenty minutes

before you appeared from the back room,
shimmering, the champagne bottle
inside my stomach coming more uncorked
with each step you took forward.
All I could do was stare.
Your fabric brushed my hand,

your breast, and you leaned in
to graze a kiss across my cheek as you passed
on the way out the door, down the stairs,

to dinner at Palmer's or to that fusion place
in Austin we'd heard about. I was in your wake,
eyes clamped shut, inhaling, and a voice said

"Do you need any help, sir?" In my palms,
on the floor, the delicate little boxes torn open
and the bottles, each one shaped
like a night someone prayed wouldn't end.
I was spraying them up—nothing illegal,
not insane, no spouts of tears—

just a man at a perfume rack
sniffing the air, thrusting his head into a mist,
uncertain what help to ask, or how, or where.

HAVING INHERITED
SELF PORTRAIT IN A CONVEX MIRROR

As if walking under a tree, the shadows of leaves

remain cast upon the mind.

One minute, the recollection of sound before meaning.

The next, digging a hole with a stick,

looking for a child's treasure.

But noise. Beginning to comprehend

that thinking is the process of whitening

like concentrating on a conversation

in an overcrowded room. Words alighting

to flock together from separate nests.

Even the adjective of a poet's name

and all the others that go with it. *Overblown.*

Abstruse. Like taking advice from a person

who has never spoken with death.

How do you honor someone like that

when you can feel the tangibility of a soul

collecting itself in the possessions

that survive it? It's not as simple

as watching a face for joy, or peering

between the blinds at troubled strangers.

Inheritance as flat as a photograph of a tree.

This relentless prayer to nature, hoarder

who collects smell and color dispassionately

as a scientist injecting rats, making studies.

All the wild predictabilities coalescing

into a library. Listening there, so many books

breathing. Someone is gone.

You keep all their things for fear

of losing them. You put them all together

like sweeping up autumn on the porch.

GOODWILL

This was right after you killed yourself.

We pulled you from the house as a mortician
pulling organs from a body. We boxed you all up.
Then a van came to clean the house
and another to take all of you away

though nothing and nobody
was willing to let go yet. There were little cries
like organs being pulled from a body.

This was right after you killed yourself.
You told us not to embalm you. They put your ashes
in a box and we took you home.
A different home. On a plane. There were forms.

About a month later, a woman at the store
took you from a hanger
in front of my eyes. She stretched you out a little
to see if you'd fit. She put you back.
The hangers were everywhere as I looked,
squeaking back and forth. Everyone

was there for you.

DOVE HUNTING
for MK

If you have to kill a symbol it's best
to do it alone,

tiptoeing between downed branches,
vigilant to the limb-crotches of evergreens
for a poorly constructed nest.
You'll strain just to notice them as birds,

having overlooked their plainness
as a nuisance of gray and brown
your entire life, and yet more difficult to see

their wingtips with your ears
when they cut the hallways of the forest
to that inborn whistling, like a sound
from a broken wheel. Someone

had to notice them first; it's become
almost easier to believe the trees themselves
are chirring in mourning.
Picture a starving man, scanning

for the trills of false pain in a wood,
paused until the air
closes around a precise tunnel

which slows such blurs for a knockdown.
You have to turn yourself off

to witness all this perception, its million eyes,
to know exactly which kind of peace
you must destroy to survive.

"THE PAST TENSE OF HANG IS HANGED."
for SBC

And here I've said for ages—literally epochs of geologic time—
"hung herself," which is actually correct
if merely connoting the brain's demand of the body,
      the choosing
to mount the self beyond gravity's rude legalese.
Lay lie laid lied: I climbed up from my storm cellar
after her suicide's meteor haymakered my Earth to shards
and I picked up whatever words were left,
festooned and suspended from bare limbs, posed arm under torso
in the blunted, scarf-draped-lampshade of new daylight.
It took encountering another creature, similarly cataclysmed,
to correct me. "She *hanged* herself," my new friend said
as we chatted on the wind-white sidewalk. I've grown
sanguine toward the method, toward her threading
a limp noose over a soffit and climbing into
      another reality,
especially considering what history offers; poor Cato
sliced his belly open, then, like unspooling cable,
ripped out his own guts when he discovered Caesar
took the Empire in one fat block. Spite wants to be violent;
I don't think I could've listened to any mammal not
similarly doomed to live beyond grammar.
      Sui cidium, in Latin;
Marcus Cato, who found his father groaning
on the bedroom floor, is a comfort; I'd be rapt
while he described his dagger's give and slide as it sank
into his Emperor on those marble steps. Sink
sunk sinked. Dive dived dove. Ken Baldwin, the guy

who plummeted from the Golden Gate and survived,
explains: "I instantly realized that everything in my life
that I'd thought was unfixable was totally fixable—
except for having jumped." If I knew she regretted it,
I wouldn't wonder what small word, what hug or touch
may have implanted itself within her elliptical orbit
        to persuade her back
toward unabated trajectory. O, O, how the fulsomeness
of choice elevates mistake to a place of near-religious
defensibility, like a baby ape night after night agog
        at the moon
until it grows to begin the business of becoming
its own moon. If all this feels aloof,

over-studied against the reality that she's really gone,
that's because it is, I am, but only insofar as I refuse
to be taken alive. Take took taken: rather than
        accepting a fate
as Roman slaves, the Jews of Masada murdered their children
and then themselves. Five kids escaped,
stumbled down from the hilltop like droplets
from a red candle. You have to know what's coming
and what came, how high this tide might rise after the last one
inhaled the shoreline and defecated its remainders
        infinity fathoms
beneath ripple and swell. "We are verbs," Hass says, "until we die.
Then we become nouns. Maybe." That's what I thought
too, Robert, before someone else's death was inside me.

I wake, I woke, I've woken. If you can mallet certain words
into plates it's just possible to rivet them together
with padded factoids and armor the inside of the skull.
Wear what you want on the outside; Hegesias gave orations
          so honest
those Greeks foolish enough to listen returned home
to their sandy bungalows and decided to die.
They just erased themselves, their hours and passions,
the exilience at surviving the midwife's ministrations to hold
          a new person,
who they owned for eternity. I'd wanted to say the past
is the opposite of killing yourself, but there are so many pasts
they radiate like electrical spokes from under our bones,
like cracks away an epicenter. There's a danger of ending up
as the character at the end of the movie, for instance,
who wears the black three-piece suit to ruminate
over how much he'll miss the voice of the dulcet beloved,
          or to feel inspired
by that 1900s writer—Russian, of course—who wrote
his suicide note as a poem in his own blood. "This is how
I want to be forgiven" is what to say to ensure you won't be;
you just leave behind a one-way street. Forgive forgave forget
forgotten. You have to know what's coming and what came,
what will arrive with its encyclopedias and crumpled hat
on your doorstep. Not knowledge, but knowing. Not dead,
but dying. I'm alive, alive, my breath readers,
beginning this sentence every way I can and praying I've learned
          not to close its eyes
just because it's curling me back, to who I am.

TAKING THE CANOE OUT AT NIGHT

Fingertips dragging the water, I lean back

under yoke and thwart, the wood of the ribs

suddenly maternal around me. Blackness

floating between stars,

I am silver needle and thread,

I am cumulonimbus breaking apart.

There could be a sun rising

behind the machinery of the face, and then

what do I see so clearly? Every so often,

gripping the haft of the paddle

and stabbing the surface lightly, just

to make sure I'm still moving.

Colin Pope grew up in the Adirondacks. His poetry has appeared in *Rattle, Ninth Letter, Slate, The Cortland Review, Willow Springs, Denver Quarterly, Los Angeles Review,* and *Best New Poets*, among others. He's the recipient of residencies and scholarships from organizations such as the Vermont Studio Center, the New York State Summer Writer's Institute, and Gemini Ink, and he has won two Academy of American Poets prizes. Colin serves on the editorial staffs of *Cimarron Review* and *Nimrod International Journal*. He holds his MFA from Texas State University and is currently a PhD candidate at Oklahoma State University in Stillwater, Oklahoma, where he lives and teaches.